THE JOY OF
hygge

Copyright © 2016 by Summersdale Publishers, Ltd.

Images © Shutterstock.

Originally published by Summersdale Publishers, Ltd. as The Art of Hygge in 2016.

First Skyhorse Publishing edition, 2017.

Skyhorse Publishing books may be purchased in bulk at special discounts for sales promotion, corporate gifts, fund-raising, or educational purposes. Special editions can also be created to specifications. For details, contact the Special Sales Department, Skyhorse Publishing, 307 West 36th Street, 11th Floor, New York, NY 10018 or info@ skyhorsepublishing.com.

Skyhorse® and Skyhorse Publishing® are registered trademarks of Skyhorse Publishing, Inc.®, a Delaware corporation.

Visit our website at www.skyhorsepublishing.com.

10 9 8 7 6 5 4 3 2

Library of Congress Cataloging-in-Publication Data is available on file.

Cover design by Jenny Zemanek
Cover photo credit: Shutterstock

Print ISBN: 978-1-5107-1811-1
Ebook ISBN: 978-1-5107-1813-5

Printed in the United States of America

THE JOY OF
hygge

How to Bring Everyday Pleasure and Danish Coziness into Your Life

JONNY JACKSON & ELIAS LARSEN

Skyhorse Publishing

Contents

Hygge

[hue ga]

What Is Hygge?

There is a reason why Denmark is one of the happiest nations on Earth, and this is in no small part due to hygge. Hygge illuminates the long, dark Scandinavian winters with candlelight and crackling hearths, and good times shared with friends and family. It's something that pervades the Danish psyche and is intrinsic to their lifestyle, all year round.

Hygge is one of those words that can't be translated into a single word or phrase, but can at once be described as a state of being and of finding joy in the simple pleasures of everyday life—from watching the sun rise to sharing a meal and good conversation with friends. The word is believed to have derived from a Norse word pertaining to well-being, but was adopted by the Danes in the eighteenth century and has been nurtured ever since.

Hygge is not something that you can buy off the shelf, but this book will help you make your life truly *hyggelig*—full of hygge—through crafting, baking, experiencing natural wonders, lingering over everyday rituals, and making the most of time spent with loved ones. Settle into your comfiest chair with a mug of something hot and delicious, and enjoy!

A RECIPE FOR HYGGE

Candlelight

An impressive log pile

A day spent in the wild

Cozy blankets

A friend to share it with

Hot chocolate

Life itself is the most wonderful fairy tale.

—Hans Christian Andersen

Chapter One

CREATING THE HYGGE MOOD AT HOME

Your home should be a sanctuary, a place where you can unwind and feel completely rested. Make your living space a delight to the senses with fragrant, fresh flowers and soft cushions and blankets made of luxurious fabrics. Lift your spirits by bathing in natural light by day and flickering candlelight and a crackling fire at night. The following simple tips will help you create a space that gives you a warm glow inside and out.

Making the Most of Natural Light

Natural light is essential to our happiness and well-being. It increases our alertness and improves mood and productivity. It also has a big impact on our body; it's how we make vitamin D, which is important for a healthy immune system and strong bones. There are numerous ways to introduce more natural light into the home; for example, swap heavy curtains for sheer panels—these could be lace or voile. Paint your walls in white, cream, or soft gray to enhance the feeling of space, and position mirrors and furniture with glossy surfaces to reflect the light back into the room. Try some of these techniques and experience for yourself how a light, airy home creates a sense of peace and serenity.

Get Cozy with Soft Furnishings

When it's cold outside, there's nothing lovelier than curling up on a sofa piled up with cushions and snuggling under a cozy blanket or quilt. Cocooned in a layer of softness, you can lose yourself in a book, watch a film, or take a nap. Dress your sofa with cushions, throws, and blankets made from merino wool, faux fur, and cashmere. These beautiful textures will bring instant warmth and luxury to any room and they're perfect for nestling into. To up the hygge factor, put on a pair of woolly socks and your comfiest pajamas.

Introduce Nature into Your Home

Nature acts like a healing balm for our body and mind and creates a relaxing, welcoming environment. There are several ways to bring nature inside. Houseplants and fresh-cut flowers are the obvious places to start. They brighten up any space and fill the air with glorious scents. For a natural look, pick a few flowers from your garden and place them into jam jars; collect pretty pebbles, shells, and driftwood; and make table decorations out of bark, leaves, berries, and pine cones—things that you have found on a country or seaside walk. Introduce warm, organic textures to your home with natural wood flooring and furniture, hand-thrown pottery, and pebbles. Natural materials are an easy way to make your home look beautiful and connected to the outdoors.

Fresh air keeps
the doctor poor.

—Danish proverb

A Breath of
Fresh Air

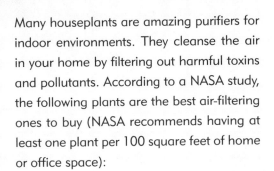

Many houseplants are amazing purifiers for indoor environments. They cleanse the air in your home by filtering out harmful toxins and pollutants. According to a NASA study, the following plants are the best air-filtering ones to buy (NASA recommends having at least one plant per 100 square feet of home or office space):

- *Aloe vera*
- Bamboo palm (*Dypsis lutescens*)
- Banana palm (*Musa basjoo*)
- Barberton daisy (*Gerbera jamesonii*)
- Boston fern (*Nephrolepis exaltata*)
- Broadleaf lady palm (*Rhapis excelsa*)
- Chinese evergreen (*Aglaonema*)
- Devil's ivy (*Epipremnum aureum*)
- Dumb cane (*Dieffenbachia*)
- Elephant ear philodendron (*Philodendron domesticum*)
- English ivy (*Hedera helix*)
- Flamingo lily (*Anthurium andraeanum*)
- Florist's daisy (*Chrysanthemum morifolium*)
- Heart-leaf philodendron (*Philodendron cordatum*)
- Kimberly queen fern (*Nephrolepis obliterata*)
- Lily turf (*Liriope muscari*)
- Moth orchids (*Phalaenopsis*)
- Peace lily (*Spathiphyllum*)

Open Fires

Relaxing in front of a log fire is one of life's great pleasures. A log fire, be it an open hearth or a modern wood burner, creates a warm, cozy atmosphere with its crackles and flickering flames. The comforting aroma of wood smoke calms and soothes, evoking primal connection and a sense of belonging. The fireplace is the meeting point and the warm heart of the home, the place where stories are shared and celebrations are toasted. Welcome family and friends to gather at the fireside and enjoy simple pleasures, such as cooking marshmallows or playing board games, or lose yourself in the reverie of watching the flames dance.

A hearth of one's own is worth gold.

—Danish proverb

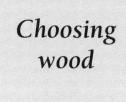

Choosing wood

When it comes to sourcing logs for your fire or wood-burning stove, there are many wood varieties to choose from, and although fire-lighting might seem like a simple affair, it's smart to have an idea of what's best for your needs. Seasoned ash, beech, birch, and yew are considered good for burning, producing a steady flame, and intense heat. In contrast, chestnut, fir, and oak are all poor burners, producing a small flame and scant heat. Many types of wood are best reserved for wood-burning stoves rather than open fires. For example, chestnut—horse and sweet—tends to spit, and poplar produces a lot of smoke. Each wood produces a different aroma, but among the most delicious scents are apple and cherry.

Eco alternatives

Compressed "eco" logs and briquettes are alternatives to traditional wood. Made from recycled materials, these are very dense and dry so they will burn well for a decent length of time.

Stacking and Storing Firewood

If you're the proud owner of an open fire or wood-burning stove, you'll know how important it is to make sure you have enough logs to see you through the winter chill. Sitting in front of a crackling fire is the epitome of hygge. But did you know that in order for your fire to burn efficiently, you need to stack your firewood properly?

First, buy logs that have been cut into short lengths (ideally 10 inches (25 cm) long) and split them to speed up drying. Then store your logs in a well-ventilated log store. Many mistakenly pile the logs on the ground and cover them with a tarp, but this encourages mold and decay to spread. Air circulation is one of the most important factors in keeping your firewood dry, and investing in a log store will pay dividends, as it allows the wood to be stacked off the ground. It should have a roof over the top and the sides should be open to the air.

Position your log store on a sheltered side of the house. To encourage air circulation, stack your wood in rows, leaving gaps between the rows. If stacking against a wall or fence, leave about 4 inches (10 cm) between the logs and the surface.

Well-stacked wood looks attractive but, crucially, it will be nice and dry by the time you need it. Dry wood burns efficiently and gives off less smoke. A warm, cozy, hyggelig household is never short of dry firewood!

Setting the Table

A beautifully set table need not be restricted to formal occasions, but is something that can be done every day to make all meal times special. It needn't be expensive; paper or linen napkins and a plain white tablecloth create a simple but effective result, as do freshly picked flowers from the garden in a jam jar, a spray of autumn leaves, or a hoard of beach finds clustered in the center of the table.

Candles and glass provide instant ambience and sparkle. Don't strive for perfection when hosting a gathering—a simple spread of cheeses, olives, and bread on a wooden board with wine, or even simply homemade buns, show that you've put love and care into your meal.

Scented candles
for a lovely aroma

Flowers from
the garden

27

Lighting Candles

There's a reason why Danes burn more candles per person than anywhere else in Europe—sharing hyggelig moments is important when braving the leaden skies and harsh Scandinavian winters, and lighting candles is one of the quickest ways of creating a warm and inviting atmosphere. Place candles, tea lights, and lanterns around your home—on the dinner table, surrounding the fireplace, and next to your computer—the more twinkly, the better! Make sure you position your candles carefully, as anything that brings fire into your home can be dangerous. Here is a list of dos and don'ts to keep you safe:

Do

- Always put candles on a heat-resistant surface. Be especially careful with tea lights, as they can become hot enough to melt plastic.

- Place candles in a proper holder so they are held upright and won't fall over.

- Position candles well away from curtains, fabrics, and any overhanging objects, and keep them out of strong drafts.

- Make sure your candles are out of reach of children and pets.

- Take special care with candles, as they turn to liquid when lit. Put them on a glass or metal holder.

- Candles that have been put out can go on smoldering for some time. Double-check that they are completely extinguished.

Don't

- Don't place a candle under a shelf, as it can easily burn the bottom of the surface.

- Never lean over a candle, as clothing and hair can easily catch fire.

- Don't leave candles burning if you leave the room.

- Avoid moving a burning candle— always snuff out the flame first.

- Never leave a burning candle or oil burner in a child's bedroom or go to sleep with a candle burning.

- When extinguishing a candle, don't blow it out, as this can send sparks and hot wax flying. Use a snuffer or a spoon to put it out.

Different waxes

Most candles are made from paraffin wax. Paraffin wax is a by-product of crude oil and is often mixed with additives to improve the burn rate. Many are concerned that burning these candles releases air pollutants and toxic black soot into the air. Alternative waxes burn more cleanly, with less soot and smoke. Beeswax is more expensive than paraffin wax, but it is a natural wax derived from honeybees. Soy wax, from soybeans, is another alternative. Less expensive than beeswax, it may be 100 percent soybean oil or soybean oil blended with other vegetable oils or waxes.

Don't forget to place candles outside your home, too. Sitting on a balcony or patio, surrounded by flickering candles, with a steaming mug of tea or coffee, is a treat that you can enjoy every day.

Essential oils

Invest in candles infused with essential oils. Aside from filling the room with beautiful aromas, essential oils can enhance our well-being and influence our thoughts, emotions, and moods. Different oils affect us in different ways. Some oils are calming, such as lavender and bergamot, and some are refreshing, such as lemon and rose. Try out some of the following if you are experiencing any of these health complaints:

- *Stress:* lavender, bergamot, vetiver, pine, and ylang-ylang

- *Insomnia:* lavender, chamomile, jasmine, rose, and sandalwood

- *Anxiety:* rose, clary sage, lemon, Roman chamomile, and sandalwood

- *Depressed mood:* peppermint, chamomile, lavender, and jasmine

- *Memory and attention problems:* sage, peppermint, and cinnamon

- *Low energy:* clove, jasmine, tea tree, rosemary, sage, and citrus

I like to hear a storm at night. It is so cozy to snuggle down among the blankets and feel that it can't get at you.

—L. M. Montgomery

HYGGE INSPIRATION

Chapter Two

ITEMS TO CRAFT FOR INSTANT HYGGE

One of the most satisfying pleasures in life is making something from scratch with your own hands. Whether you're crafting a cute woolly hat with a pom-pom or sewing a fluffy pair of slippers, a handmade item oozes character and originality. The following pages reveal how to make super-cozy accessories and thoughtful gifts, which will fill you with hygge happiness.

A good handicraft rests on a golden foundation.

—Danish proverb

Lavender Bags

Lavender has been used for its healing properties for thousands of years, and its fragrance can be relaxing and restorative. Lavender bags are easy to make and are useful in many different ways. Try tucking one in a drawer or wardrobe to keep your clothes and sheets smelling fresh, or pop one under your pillow to encourage a peaceful night's sleep. You could even keep one in your handbag or pocket to help you de-stress with its calming aroma when you're having a busy day.

What you'll need

Pretty fabric

Scissors

Pins

Needle and thread

Dried lavender

Optional extra: ribbon

Instructions

Cut out two rectangles of fabric measuring 6 x 4.5 inches (16 x 11.5 cm).

Pin the two rectangles together, patterned sides facing each other.

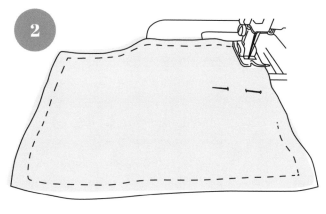

Starting about ³/₄ inch (2 cm) from the edge of one of the short sides, sew all the way round the rectangle, stopping roughly ³/₄ inch (2 cm) from the other corner.

3

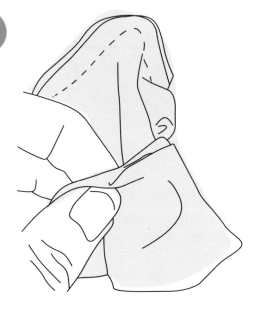

Cut off the corners and turn the rectangle the right way around, pushing the fabric through the gap you've left (you can use the end of a pencil or a paint brush to push out the corners so they're pointy).

4

Iron the seam across the gap so it's nice and straight.

Fill with dried lavender (you can buy this online or through a local lavender farm), or dry your own if you have access to a lavender bush.

5

If you'd like to hang up your bag, place a loop of ribbon halfway across the top edge of the gap and sew across the gap, backstitching over the ribbon to make sure it stays in place.

Ta-dah! — your own gorgeous lavender bag!

Felt Slippers

Slippers are essential attire for pajama days. No slippers? No problem! Show your feet some love with these felt slippers, which will keep you feeling toasty all year round.

What you'll need

Paper

$19\frac{1}{2}$ x $19\frac{1}{2}$ inches (50 x 50 cm) square of wool felt

Scissors

Dressmaker's chalk or fabric marker

Strong thread, such as silk or polyester

Large darning needle

Instructions

Enlarge and cut out the template below so that it is twice as wide and about an inch longer than the sole of your shoe—either scan it and print it or enlarge it on a photocopier.

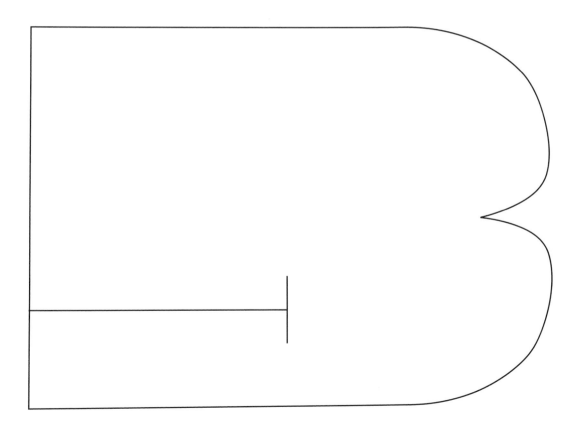

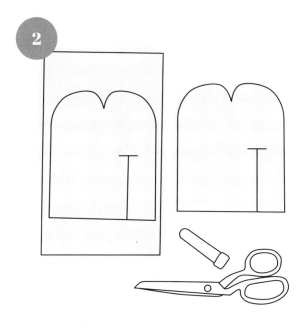

Trace the template onto your felt and cut carefully, including the T shape.

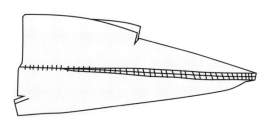

Fold the felt in half lengthwise, and stitch the seam of the toe. Pinch the heel seams together and sew from the top of the slipper to approximately $3/4$ inch (2 cm) from the heel and carefully snip into the heel to create a small flap.

4

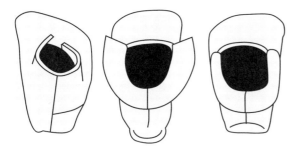

Tuck this flap in and sew it securely. Then, turn the slipper inside out and tidy the edges of the flap by rounding them with your scissors.

You can either finish there or fold the sides down to the ankle and sew these against the slipper.

When sewing the other slipper, remember to flip the template so the T is on the opposite side.

For extra hygge, customize with pom-poms, lace, or home-made felt flowers, or design them to match your favorite pajamas—the sky's the limit!

Pom-Pom for a Beanie Hat

Upcycle one of your tired woolly beanies with a bit of hygge cheer! Pom-poms are great fun to make—and why stop with one pom-pom when you could have ten, in different colors?

What you'll need

Cardboard

Scissors

Yarn

Needle and thread

Instructions

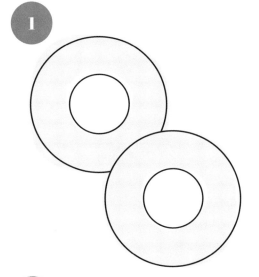

1

Cut out two cardboard discs of the same size (the bigger the disc, the bigger the pom-pom).

Cut a small hole in the middle of each disc and lay them on top of each other. Make sure the hole is big enough to pass the yarn through.

2

Loop the yarn through the holes and around the outer edges of the discs, holding it in place with your fingers to begin with to make sure it does not unravel.

3

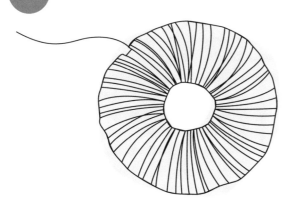

Repeat until the discs are completely and evenly covered. Place the scissors between the two discs of cardboard and cut through the yarn that's around the outer edge.

4

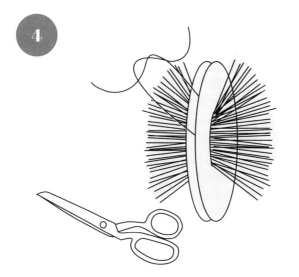

Carefully wrap a long piece of thread between each disc around the yarn that's between the two discs and tie a knot to hold your pom-pom together. (Leave enough thread to sew the pom-pom onto your hat.) Once the yarn is securely tied, cut the cardboard and pull it away from the pom-pom.

5

Fluff up your pom-pom and give it a trim with scissors, if necessary, to make it perfectly round.

Sew the pom-pom onto your hat and go out into the crisp, cold air with a jaunty spring in your step.

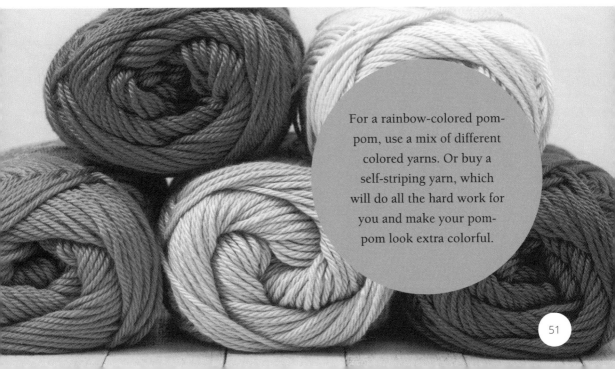

For a rainbow-colored pom-pom, use a mix of different colored yarns. Or buy a self-striping yarn, which will do all the hard work for you and make your pom-pom look extra colorful.

Mug Cozy

Make your favorite mug a smart little jacket for winter—not only will it look very fetching, but it will also keep your hot chocolate steaming a little bit longer. It's also a genius way to upcycle a woolly sock!

What you'll need

Mug

Ruler

Woolly sock

Scissors

Needle and thread

Fabric glue (optional)

Optional extras: buttons, felt shapes, mini pom-poms, sequins

Instructions

1

Choose your favorite mug and measure its height.

2

Cut the sock at the ankle and keep the top section.

Turn the top section of the sock inside out and hem the seams securely with the thread.

3

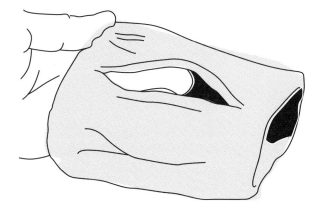

Turn the sock right-side out and carefully cut a slit for the mug handle. Overstitch the edges or use the fabric glue to prevent fraying. If using glue, be sparing so it will dry clear, and leave to dry for the time it suggests on the bottle. Then fit your cozy over the mug.

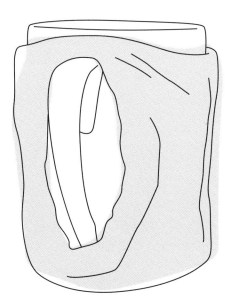

Give your mug cozy some extra hygge by adding decorative flourishes with buttons, felt, or whatever your imagination permits. And why stop there? Make a cozy for your flask in the same way so it doesn't feel left out!

Fairy-Light Lanterns

Add a little sparkle to your life by creating some fairy-light lanterns. Fairy lights are a wonderful way to create a special atmosphere. They cast a romantic, whimsical glow and add a touch of magic to any room. These lanterns take minutes to make and create a stunning backdrop for a party or a cozy night in.

What you'll need

1–3 large mason jars

1–3 strings of LED battery-operated fairy lights

A piece of burlap big enough to cover the battery pack

Adhesive tape

Instructions

- Take one string of fairy lights and disguise the battery pack with a small piece of burlap. Carefully drop the battery pack into the bottom of a mason jar (make sure the on–off button is facing up so you can easily reach in and turn the lights off).*

- Spread the fairy lights inside the jar so they fill the space. (You may need to use several strings of fairy lights if you are using a very large jar.)

- Tape the top of the light string to the inside of the lid and screw the lid back on the jar.

- Decorate the jar with red ribbon, if desired, or leave it plain for a more rustic look.

- Place the mason jar(s) on a tray or mantelpiece and arrange pine cones, ornaments, and confetti stars around the base.

- Stand back and be dazzled by your creation.

*Alternatively, buy a string of fairy lights with a battery pack small enough to tape to the underside of the jar lid. Tie a thick ribbon or piece of fabric around the neck of the jar to hide the battery pack from view.

HYGGE INSPIRATION

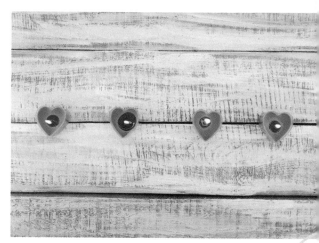

Chapter Three

DECORATING THE HOME

Hygge is about instilling a feeling of contentment and happiness, and doing this in the home doesn't require spending a fortune. Decorate your home with items that bring you joy, such as fresh flowers and pine cones collected on country walks. Also, add items that conjure up happy memories, such as paper snowflakes and winter bunting. These simple touches create a home that's warm and inviting. You'll know you've got it right when your guests smile as they walk through the door!

Fresh Flowers

Nothing nurtures the heart and soul more than fresh flowers. Fill your home with blooms that make you feel happy—bold tulips, romantic roses, and vibrant daffodils—and choose scents that make you smile, such as sweet hyacinths or fragrant lilies. Hygge is about cherishing yourself, so don't wait for someone to buy you flowers; head to your local florist or farmers' market and treat yourself to a bunch of your favorites. Even better: pick sweet peas, lavender, and peonies straight from your garden or window box. Don't worry if you don't have enough vases—you can use jugs, jam jars, glass bottles, Mason jars, and even mugs. Whether it's a bouquet or a single striking stem, place the flowers where you can see them every day and they can work their magic.

Beauty without virtue is a rose without scent.

—Danish proverb

Paper Snowflakes

Answer your wishes for a snowy day by making these paper snowflakes. They are simple to create and will transform your home into a winter wonderland. Hang them from the ceiling, thread them to make a garland, or make your very own snow scene by attaching them to windows. Making paper snowflakes will transport you straight back to the magic and wonder of Christmas when you were small.

What you'll need

Square white paper (lightweight craft paper works best)

Sharp scissors or scalpel

Instructions

- Take one piece of square paper. Fold the paper in half diagonally to make a triangle.

- Fold the triangle in half again so the two pointy corners meet. Fold your triangle in thirds (make sure the sides match up).

- Remove the two bottom points by cutting straight across the shortest edge of the triangle.

- Cut away shapes along the edges of the folded paper. Then unfold the paper gently to reveal your masterpiece!

Experiment with different paper sizes and types.

Create a Nature Display

Do you always come back from a walk with your pockets full of unusual stones, twigs, and leaves? If you're stumped for what to do with your finds when you get back home, try making a nature display. It's great fun sorting through your findings and thinking of fun ways to display them. You could arrange a collection of shells and driftwood from the beach or place interesting rocks and pebbles in glass jars. Berry branches and pine cones look striking when arranged in large vases or can be hung from the ceiling like a giant mobile. Don't limit your display to a table in the corner. Experiment by arranging your treasures in a tray or a box, or make a feature of them on a mantelpiece or shelf. This is a great way to reconnect with the wonder of nature, and the beauty of it is that the whole family can get involved. Happy collecting!

Things to collect

Woodland and countryside:
Moss, pine cones, hazelnuts, twigs, fallen tree bark, chestnuts, sycamore helicopters, and acorns

Garden:
Dried sunflower heads, seed pods, dandelion clocks, stones, leaves, petals, squashes, and gourds

Beach:
Shells (without creatures inside), sea snail egg cases, dried seaweed, seagull feathers, mermaid's purses, and sharks' teeth

Pumpkin Carving

When October is drawing to a close, it means one thing: it's time to put on spooky costumes and make lanterns out of pumpkins! Pumpkin carving is a fun group activity for family and friends.

The best bit? When a lit candle is placed inside the pumpkin, it casts a beautiful warm glow that will ward off werewolves and witches.

How to carve a pumpkin

- Cut off the stem at the top of the pumpkin— it's tougher than you might think, so use a sharp knife.

- Scoop out the flesh and seeds—children love this messy bit. Keep the seeds for planting.

- Draw or trace a face or design onto the pumpkin with a felt-tip pen. Cut out the patterns using a sharp knife.

- Place some tea lights (real or electric) inside the pumpkin. Light them and place the stem back on, like a lid.

- Leave your carved pumpkin outside on the doorstep, a windowsill, or a gatepost to light up a cold, dark evening and delight visitors and passers-by.

Winter Bunting

Homemade bunting is a quick and fun way to bring a party feel to any indoor space. It creates a gorgeous border in a room and adds a touch of rustic charm. It's easy to make, and you can use all sorts of odds and ends to create your bunting— scraps of paper, pieces of fabric, old clothes, and even plastic and paper bags. Unleash your creative side and have a cozy craft day at home.

What you'll need

Thin cardboard

Pretty material and fabrics

Glue, or needle and thread

Ribbon, string, or twine

Drawing pins to hang the bunting (optional)

Scissors

Instructions

- Make a triangle template out of cardboard.

- Use the template to cut lots of triangles from your chosen material (wintry designs, such as snowflakes, icicles, and pine trees, work well, as do warm patterns, such as tartan).

- Glue or stitch the triangles to a length of ribbon, string, or rustic twine.

- The trickiest part of the whole process is choosing where to hang your bunting! It looks great in bedrooms and adds a quirky edge to kitchens and living rooms. You can hang it on walls, attach it to shelves, or use it as a garland for a mantelpiece—just be careful it's not too near the fire.

- Once you've hung your bunting, invite some friends over to admire your handiwork (this is the perfect excuse for a night of board games, drinks, and snacks!).

HYGGE INSPIRATION

Chapter Four

COMFORTING RECIPES FOR COZY NIGHTS IN

Hygge is about sharing good times with the people you love, and one of the best ways of doing this is to sit down together for a meal or tea and cake and discuss the big (and little) things in life. Food calms, comforts, hugs, and heals, and the following recipes will bring instant hygge happiness.

Iced Vanilla Cookies

These mouth-watering cookies will fill your home with the sweet aroma of vanilla as they bake. Fresh from the oven, they are buttery, warm, and gooey in the middle. The perfect melt-in-the-mouth treat to offer guests. *(Makes approx. 24 cookies)*

Ingredients

3½ ounces (100 g) unsalted butter, softened at room temperature

3½ ounces (100 g) superfine granulated sugar

1 medium free-range egg, lightly beaten

1 tsp vanilla extract

9¾ ounces (275 g) plain flour

To decorate:

14 ounces (400 g) powdered sugar

3–4 tbsp water

2–3 drops food coloring

Method

Preheat the oven to 375°F (190°C, Gas 5).

Place the butter and sugar in a bowl and beat until combined. Beat in the egg and vanilla extract, a little at a time. Stir in the flour until the mixture forms a dough.

Lightly flour a work surface and roll the dough out to a thickness of ¾ inches (1 cm). Cut cookies out of the dough using cookie cutters and place onto a baking tray that has been lined with parchment paper.

Bake the cookies until pale golden-brown (around 8–10 minutes). Leave to harden for 5 minutes and transfer to a wire rack.

While the cookies are cooling, make the icing. Sift the powdered sugar into a large mixing bowl and stir in the water, as per the instructions given on the packet, until the mixture is smooth. Stir in the food coloring and spread the icing onto the cookies using a knife or decorate using a piping bag. Set aside until the icing hardens.

Cinnamon Hot Chocolate

If hygge were a drink, it would be rich hot chocolate. This sumptuous hot chocolate recipe is a warming hug in a mug. (*Serves 1*)

Ingredients

1 tbsp cocoa powder

1 tbsp sugar

¼ tsp ground cinnamon

½ tsp vanilla extract

2 tbsp and ¾ cup (180 ml) milk (dairy or nut)

To serve (optional):

Cream

Marshmallows

Cinnamon

Method

Mix together the cocoa powder, sugar, cinnamon, vanilla, and 2 tbsp of milk in a mug. Use a fork or a mini whisk until the mixture resembles a thick syrup.

Over a medium heat, warm the rest of the milk until it begins to bubble, then pour it into the mug with the chocolate syrup and stir thoroughly.

For added indulgence, serve with a dollop of cream or marshmallows and a sprinkle of cinnamon.

Roasted Chestnuts

Roasted chestnuts are the perfect excuse to cuddle up with your loved ones by the fire. Cooked to perfection, their pale insides become nutty, creamy, and surprisingly sweet. Serve as they are or dip them in spiced melted butter. *(Serves 4–6)*

Ingredients

2¼ lbs (1 kg) chestnuts

For the spiced butter:

2 ounces (60 g) unsalted butter

1 cinnamon stick

Pinch of nutmeg, salt, and sugar

Method

Heat the oven to 400°F (200°C, Gas 6).

Lay the chestnuts on their flat sides and use a sharp knife to cut a long slit or a cross in the curved shell (when you roast them, the steam will escape and they won't explode).

Place in a roasting tin in a single layer, flat-side down, and bake until the skin splits open. This should take around 30 minutes.

When the chestnuts are cool enough to handle, peel away the tough outer skin and pop the sweet white kernel into your mouth.

For the spiced butter:

Melt the butter over a low heat and stir in the spices, salt, and sugar. Once melted, remove the cinnamon stick and transfer the mixture to a small dish for dipping.

To bake on a fire:

Place the prepared chestnuts in a cast-iron frying pan or a skillet in a single layer.

Position the pan in the glowing embers of the fire.

Turn the chestnuts over from time to time so they cook evenly. They will take 5–10 minutes to cook.

Berry Jam

Hygge is all about doing little things that make you happy, such as making homemade jam. After an hour in the kitchen immersed in stirring, bottling, and labeling, the berries are transformed into jars of fruity loveliness, ready to be slathered onto hot-buttered toast or a scone. Sticky and sweet, this jam will give you a warm glow of satisfaction that comes from making something with your own hands. For ultimate hygge, pick your own berries for making jam! *(Makes 2 small jars)*

Ingredients

17½ ounces (500 g) mixed seasonal berries, such as blackberries, boysenberries, and raspberries

10½ ounces (300 g) sugar

1½ tbsp lemon juice

Method

Place the berries in a large saucepan, bring slowly to boiling point, and then simmer for 5 minutes.

Add in the sugar, stir, and leave to simmer for 10–15 minutes. Remove the pan from the heat and stir in the lemon juice. Pour the jam into sterilized jars and seal with a lid. Leave to set and cool. The jam will keep for at least a year if stored in a cool, dry cupboard, but once opened, it must be stored in a fridge.

Gingerbread House

Christmas is the high season for hygge, and few things conjure up the magic of Christmas more than a gingerbread house. Constructing a gingerbread house takes time, but the whole family will be absorbed for hours and children will love using their imaginations to decorate the house with snowy icing and sweets. *(Makes 1 house)*

Ingredients

6¼ ounces (175 g) unsalted butter

7 ounces (200 g) light-brown soft sugar

1 tsp lemon zest

1½ tbsp lemon juice

5 fluid ounces (150 g) molasses

2 eggs, beaten

13¼ ounces (375 g) plain flour

2 tsp baking powder

1 tbsp ground ginger

2 tsp ground allspice

For the icing:

6 egg whites

3¾ lbs (1.75 kg) powdered sugar, sifted

Method

Make templates for the roof and walls of the house by cutting shapes from thin cardboard. You will need a side wall (4.75 x 7.75 inches); an end wall (4.75 x 5 in); a triangular gable (4.75 x 3 x 3 inches); and a roof rectangle (4.75 x 9 inches).

Match the long side of the triangular gable piece (4.75 inches) to one of the 4.75-inch sides of the end wall and tape together.

Make the gingerbread mixture by creaming the butter and sugar until light and fluffy. Add the lemon zest, lemon juice, and molasses. Mix in two beaten eggs. Sift the flour, baking powder, and spices into the mixture and combine well to form a dough. Wrap the dough in baking parchment and put in the fridge for 1 hour.

Divide the dough into six pieces, making two pieces slightly larger than the others. Roll out the four smaller pieces on a lightly floured surface and cut out two side walls and two end walls with triangular gables (see approximate measurements above). Roll out the remaining dough and cut out two roof pieces.

Assorted sweets for decoration such as:

White chocolate buttons (roof tiles), licorice pieces, mini fruit snacks, gum drops, and colored sprinkles

Place the gingerbread shapes onto greased baking trays and bake in a preheated oven at 375°F (190°C, Gas 5) for 10 minutes until crisp. Remove from the oven and leave to set for a few minutes. Transfer to wire racks and leave overnight to harden.

To make the icing, lightly whisk two egg whites and gradually beat in approximately one third of the powdered sugar until the mixture is smooth and forms firm peaks.

Now you're ready to construct the house. Spread or pipe a 9-inch line of icing onto a cake board and press one of the side walls firmly into this so that it stands upright. You may need to pipe a little more icing along either side of the wall to give it extra support. Take an end wall and ice both the side edges. Spread or pipe a line of icing on the board at a right angle to the first wall and press the end wall firmly into the icing. Repeat this process with the remaining side and end walls to form the walls of your house. Leave to harden for at least 2 hours before adding the roof.

To construct the roof, spread or pipe a thick layer of icing on top of all the walls and press the roof pieces into the icing, making sure the roof overlaps the walls to make the eaves. Fix the two roof pieces together by piping or spreading a little icing along the crest of the roof. Leave overnight to harden.

Now you're ready to make some icing to decorate the house. Lightly whisk four egg whites and mix in the remaining powdered sugar. Use the icing to glue various sweets onto the house to create a door, windows, and roof tiles. Add icing to the roof to create snow and finish with a dusting of icing sugar.

Fruit Crumble

Homemade fruit crumble is the ultimate comfort food and is guaranteed to keep the cold at bay. This cinnamon-infused apple and blackberry crumble has a rich, golden oaty topping for a satisfying crunch. Serve it with ice cream or dollops of custard. (*Serves 4*)

Ingredients

5 apples, peeled and cut into cubes

5¼ ounces (150 g) blackberries

6 tbsp light-brown soft sugar

½ tsp cinnamon

1 tsp vanilla extract

For the topping:

3½ ounces (100 g) plain flour

2 tbsp brown sugar

¼ tsp cinnamon

1¾ ounces (50 g) unsalted butter, chilled and cubed

4 tbsp oats

Method

Preheat the oven to 350°F (180°C, Gas 4).

Place the chopped apples with the blackberries, sugar, cinnamon, and vanilla extract in a heavy-bottomed pot. Mix well and cook for 5 minutes over a medium heat.

Meanwhile, make the topping by mixing the flour, sugar, and cinnamon in a small bowl. Rub the butter into the mix until it resembles breadcrumbs, then mix in the oats.

Spoon the fruit mixture into the ovenproof dish and sprinkle the crumble on top. Bake for 15–20 minutes until golden and bubbling.

Hot Spiced Fruit Punch

Hygge is about the soft glow of candlelight, good times spent with the people you love, getting cozy in front of the fire, and the occasional clink of glasses as they're topped up with something warm and delicious. This recipe, infused with exotic spices and winter fruits, is like a warm hug in a glass. (*Serves 6–8*)

Ingredients

1 orange

10 cloves, whole

5 liters of unsweetened fruit juice—choose a mixture of juices, such as orange, red grape, pineapple, apple, and cranberry

1 cup (250 ml) water

¼ tsp ground cinnamon

¼ tsp ground nutmeg

1 cinnamon stick (plus extra to serve)

1 star anise (plus extra to serve)

1 apple

Handful of cranberries

Juice of 1 lemon

Method

Cut the orange in half, then push the cloves into the peel of one half.

Pour your mixture of fruit juices making up a liter into a saucepan with the water. Then stir in the ground cinnamon and nutmeg with a wooden spoon.

Add the half of the orange filled with cloves into the pan together with the cinnamon stick and star anise. Heat the mixture on a stove and let it simmer for 20 minutes. Pour the mixture from the pan through a sieve and into a bowl.

Discard the orange and the whole spices in the sieve. Slice up the other half of the orange and the apple. Add the slices to the bowl together with the cranberries and the juice of your lemon.

Use a jug or a ladle to pour some punch into a glass. Now stoke the fire, admire the frosty scenery outside, put your feet up, and relax . . .

Mulled Wine

Guaranteed to warm you from the inside and takes only a few minutes to prepare. The heady aroma of spices makes this a wonderful seasonal party drink. (*Serves 8*)

Ingredients

1 bottle of red wine

1 orange, quartered

2 ounces (60 g) demerara or brown sugar

1 cinnamon stick

1 tsp grated nutmeg

1 bay leaf, fresh

2 whole cloves

2 star anise

To serve (optional):

Orange slices studded with cloves

Cinnamon sticks

Star anise

Method

Pour a quarter of the red wine into a saucepan. Stir in the orange pieces, demerara or brown sugar, and spices.

Heat gently to a simmer until the sugar has dissolved.

Taste for sweetness and spiciness, and add more sugar or spices to taste.

Bring to a boil for a few minutes, allowing the spices to infuse until the mixture starts to resemble syrup.

Reduce to a gentle heat and add the rest of the wine and the star anise and heat through for a few minutes. Strain into heatproof glasses or mugs. For extra spice, serve with orange slices studded with cloves, cinnamon sticks, and star anise.

Mulled Cider

Impossible to resist with its flavors of citrus, rum, clove, and apple, this cider recipe is a perfect way to use up windfall apples. *(Serves 8)*

Ingredients

8 cups (2 liters) cider

2 apples studded with cloves

4 cinnamon sticks

5 whole allspice berries

Zest of 1 orange

2 measures of rum (dark is best)

To serve (optional):

Slices of apple

Star anise

Cinnamon sticks

Method

Place all the ingredients into a large saucepan and heat to a gentle simmer for half an hour. Be careful not to let it boil.

Take off the heat, strain, and transfer to a heatproof bowl before ladling into heatproof glasses or mugs.

Serve with apple slices, star anise, and cinnamon sticks.

Butternut Squash Soup

Welcome yourself home with a big bowl of creamy butternut squash soup. Easy to make and very nutritious, this dinner-time treat is the equivalent of a cozy knitted jumper (plus you can reheat it for lunch!). *(Serves 2)*

Ingredients

1 large or 2 small butternut squashes

Handful of fresh, chopped sage leaves

Freshly ground black pepper

1–2 tbsp olive oil

2 onions, chopped

1 quart (1 liter) chicken or vegetable stock

To serve (optional):

Crème fraîche

Pumpkin seeds

A sprinkle of fresh thyme leaves

A sliver of blue cheese

Salt and pepper

Method

Preheat the oven to 350°F (180°C, Gas 4).

Deseed the butternut squash (no need to peel it) and cut into large cubes. Mix with the sage leaves, black pepper, and olive oil. Tip the mixture into a roasting tin and bake in the oven for around 35–45 minutes.

While the squash is cooking, sauté the onions in a large saucepan until translucent. When the butternut squash has softened and the sage leaves are crispy, add the mix to the onions and cover with the stock.

Simmer for 30 minutes, then remove from the heat, season to taste, and blend using a hand blender until smooth (for a really silky soup, blend).

Decorate with fresh thyme leaves and pumpkin seeds on top of swirls of crème fraîche and a sliver of blue cheese. Add salt and pepper to taste. Serve with crusty bread.

Popcorn

Whether sweet or savory, popcorn is a perennial favorite—nothing tastes better when you want to chill out on the sofa and have a movie night. *(Serves 4)*

Ingredients

1 tbsp sunflower or
 vegetable oil

1¾ ounces (50 g)
 popping corn

Serving options:

Powdered sugar, honey,
 salt, butter, or
 chocolate

Method

Place the oil and kernels in a large, heavy-based pan with a tight-fitting lid. (Using a heavy-based pan will ensure the kernels don't burn during cooking.) Note: Only fill the pan one-quarter full of corn kernels so that there is room for them to expand.

Cook with the lid on over a medium heat, shaking the pan occasionally, until the kernels start to "pop" and burst out of their skins.

Once the popping has died down, remove the pan from the heat and pour into a large bowl.

While the popcorn is still warm, sprinkle it with powdered sugar or drizzled honey, or a little salt. Alternatively, add a little butter to the pan and stir it into the popcorn as it melts. For a real treat, drizzle the popcorn with melted chocolate and leave to set.

Chocolate Fondue

Everyone loves a chocolate fondue. This easy-to-make dessert is the perfect excuse to gather everyone together for a fun, sociable evening. Chunks of fresh strawberry, pineapple, and banana make delicious dunkers for the rich, creamy sauce. Whether you're hanging out with friends or planning a romantic meal at home for two, this heavenly chocolate fondue is sure to impress! *(Serves 4)*

Ingredients

3¾ ounces (110 g) sugar

½ cup (110 ml) water

14 ounces (400 g) chocolate (dark, milk, or white)

To serve:

Selection of fruit (e.g., strawberries, banana, grapes, pineapple)

Marshmallows

Method

Gently heat the sugar and water in a saucepan until the sugar melts and forms a syrup.

Place a heatproof bowl over a pan of simmering water and add the chocolate, breaking it into pieces. (Do not let the base of the bowl touch the water as this can cause the chocolate to seize and go lumpy.)

Add the syrup to the chocolate and stir with a wooden spoon to form a smooth sauce. The sauce will be very hot so leave to cool a little before serving.

To serve, dip bite-sized pieces of fresh fruit or marshmallows into the sauce. You can add extra flavors to the sauce too, such as some orange zest, a teaspoon of peppermint extract, the contents of a vanilla pod, or a tablespoon or two of Irish cream liqueur.

Spiced Banana Bread

Like manna from heaven, spiced banana bread with a slick of fresh butter is a delicious treat either for breakfast, afternoon tea, or dessert. *(Makes 12–15 slices)*

Ingredients

2 ounces (55 g)
   unsalted butter

7 ounces (200 g)
   brown sugar

1 egg, beaten

3 overripe bananas,
   mashed

8²/₃ ounces (250 g)
   self-raising flour

1 teaspoon salt

2 tsp mixed spices
   (a pinch of nutmeg
   and cinnamon)

1³/₄ ounces (50 g) dark
   chocolate, grated

To serve (optional):

Slices of banana

Butter

Method

Preheat the oven to 350°F (180°C, Gas 4).

Grease a 7.75 x 4 inch loaf tin or line with parchment paper.

Cream the butter and sugar with an electric whisk or wooden spoon.

Add the beaten egg and mashed bananas into the mixture.

Using a spatula or wooden spoon, fold in the flour, salt, spices, and grated dark chocolate.

Pour the mixture into the loaf tin and cook for 1 hour.

If the top starts to look too brown during cooking, place parchment paper on the top until the bread is ready so that it doesn't burn.

Serve with butter, sliced banana, or whatever takes your fancy!

HYGGE INSPIRATION

Chapter Five

SEASONAL OUTDOOR ACTIVITIES

Hygge isn't just about shutting out the cold and snuggling by the fire. This chapter offers ideas for making the most of the great outdoors and reconnecting with nature, whatever the weather.

Winter Beach Walks

Coastal weather in the winter months can mean high winds, stormy seas, and biting temperatures, but it makes the seaside an exhilarating destination for walking, playing games, beachcombing, or just a place to enjoy being outside in the open air. Wrap up against the cold and perhaps take a flask of something hot.

Winter storms offer up all sorts of interesting flotsam and jetsam, which makes winter one of the best times of year for beachcombing. Wander down at low tide and sift through the shingle for sharks' teeth, or take a kite or bat and ball and make the most of the vast, empty space. Check the tide times before setting out, especially if you're going to a part of the coast with limited access at high tide; wear shoes with grips to avoid slipping on wet rocks or loose shingle; and take a pair of binoculars, as you might be lucky enough to spot some coastal birds or a gray seal bobbing in the water.

Fruit Picking in the Hedgerows

Autumn hedgerows are bursting with delicious edible treasure; fruits such as blackberries and elderberries are just asking to be picked. So grab a bag or a basket and harvest the wild hedgerows. Foraging is a great way for the whole family to reconnect with nature while enjoying the last of the fine weather. Pluck blackberries from bushes to make a fruit crumble, pick bunches of ripe elderberries for a delicious sweet jelly, or in some regions, you can collect sloes to make gin. Make sure you take a guidebook or expert with you so you know what's safe to eat, and *never* eat anything you're unsure of.

Picnics

Picnics are most frequently associated with summertime, but the summer has its downsides: crunchy sand in your sandwiches, having to swipe away curious beasties, and making a run for it when that ominous little gray cloud becomes a biblical downpour . . . So why not try a picnic in the cooler months, on a bright autumn or winter day?

Food brings people together and never more so than on a picnic. Sitting on a blanket, sharing food and conversation is a wonderful hyggelig experience. Why not organize a picnic and ask everyone to bring a dish to share? Head to a beautiful setting, such as a beach, park, forest, or nature reserve, and spread out plenty of blankets— take extra layers in case it turns chilly. Let everyone help themselves to platefuls of delicious food, then sit back and relax.

Remember: a picnic doesn't need to be complicated to be a success. Keep things simple but warming with hot soup, chili, or stew in a flask, baked potatoes wrapped in foil, and hot chocolate and cookies for dessert. . . . Food always tastes better when eaten al fresco!

Picnics can also be impromptu affairs— eat your work lunch in the park, take your dinner to the beach, or head out on a road trip with flasks of soup. Wherever you are and whomever you're with, what makes a picnic special is savoring the surroundings, the food, and the people you're sharing it with.

Bike Rides

Few activities inspire a greater sense of freedom than a bike ride. It's an excellent form of low-impact exercise and will give you a thrill as you cycle along tracks and freewheel down hills—like you used to when you were a child.

Enjoy the fresh air as it ruffles your hair and the warmth of the sun on your face. Connect with your body as you power the pedals. There's no better way to travel!

I felt my lungs inflate with the onrush of scenery . . . I thought, "This is what it is to be happy."

—Sylvia Plath

Woodland Walks

To reconnect with the simple things in life, wrap up, don your walking boots, and head to the woods. Trees provide shelter for all sorts of animals, so woods are fantastic places to look and listen for wildlife. Perhaps you'll hear the call of a cuckoo or owl, or see the tracks of a fox or badger. Maybe you'll come across a carpet of bluebells in springtime, or find shiny conkers scattered beneath the branches of a horse chestnut tree in autumn. Woods are exciting places to explore. You can turn the walk into a scavenger hunt—there are so many things to pick up and collect, such as pine cones, leaves, acorns, and feathers. Tap into your playful side by hugging a tree or balancing on logs. Being in the woods is a great way to recharge your batteries. Trees emit aromatics and chemicals that enhance our well-being and encourage us to relax. Head to the woods and soak up the revitalizing atmosphere.

Fun in the Snow

Hygge is found in small moments of happiness, such as waking up to the first frost of the year, or, even better, the first snowfall. Opening the curtains to see a world blanketed in glittering, powdery snow is breathtaking. The crunch of snow underfoot is the only sound in the thick silence . . . until the fun begins! Snow is a great excuse to act like a child again—to have snowball fights, build a snowman, make snow angels, and go sledding. When the gleeful shrieks and laughter have died down, take the whole family out for a stroll and marvel at how the landscape has been transformed into a winter wonderland, glistening with snow and ice. Then head home, with rosy cheeks and big smiles, to hot drinks by the fire, a family film, and a head full of happy memories.

Bonfires

Building a bonfire is the ultimate outdoor hyggelig activity. Make it an event by inviting friends for some campfire cooking. Wrap potatoes in tin foil and tuck them in the embers until the insides are soft and fluffy, then serve with butter. For dessert, roast marshmallows on long twigs or make everyone's favorite: bonfire bananas (roasted bananas that have been slit in half lengthwise and stuffed with pieces of chocolate). Sit back and enjoy the feeling of complete coziness and contentment as you gather around a crackling fire.

How to build a bonfire

- Find a safe area away from fences, trees, bushes, buildings, and any household trash or garden waste.

- Dig a shallow pit to contain the fire. It should be approximately 4 inches (10 cm) deep and about 1 yard (1 meter) wider than you'd like your fire to be.

- Place bricks or large stones around the edge of the pit to contain the fire.

- Put some fire lighters in the center of the pit and add a bundle of tinder on top (you can use wood shavings, newspaper, twigs, bark, grass, dry leaves, and even moss).

- Arrange dry kindling over the tinder at 45-degree angles, meeting in the middle to form the shape of a tepee. Leave some gaps in the kindling so the oxygen can reach the tinder.

- Place a lit match under your tinder or drop it inside the tepee. The tinder should catch light, followed by the kindling.

- When the kindling tepee collapses, add logs to fuel the fire.

- At the end of the evening, make sure you put the fire out completely. This takes longer than you think, so leave at least 20 minutes for this. Sprinkle water over the fire to put out the embers and, when cool, pile some dirt or sand on top.

- Don't allow children near the fire without adult supervision.

Toasting marshmallows in front of the fire

Crisp on the outside and gloriously gooey on the inside, there is nothing more hyggelig than toasted marshmallows! Relive your childhood by placing a marshmallow on the end of a kebab stick and hunkering down by your fireplace or firepit to roast the marshmallow until it turns golden. You can either squish the marshmallow between two graham crackers or plop the whole thing straight into your mouth. Have the wet wipes ready for sticky fingers and watch out—the yummy goodness will be hot inside!

Natural Wonders

Watching the sunset

There is something inherently powerful and sacred about sunsets. These wonders of nature have inspired poets and writers for centuries. We could all benefit from taking the time to savor a sunset. Pick a clear day and find a spot with a view of the western horizon. Wrap up warm and arrive in plenty of time to soak up the experience. Sit with a friend or loved one and watch in awe as the sun sinks lower and the sky shimmers with hues of pink, orange, and gold. Practice this mindful ritual on a regular basis—it's an easy way to infuse some beauty and wonder into your day.

Stargazing

A clear night is the perfect time to explore the wonders of the night sky. All you need is a star map and some binoculars to spot some stunning celestial objects. Download an evening sky map from the Internet and buy or borrow a compass to help you navigate the night sky. It's best to stargaze away from cities and areas with light pollution—try a park, a hill, or a beach. Seek out the North Star and constellations, such as the Big Dipper, Orion, and Cassiopeia. Look out for distant planets and meteors, too. Make sure you take a blanket to lie on, plenty of warm clothes, and a flask of hot drink to keep big and little stargazers happy!

There they stand, the innumerable stars, shining in order like a living hymn, written in light.

—Nathaniel Parker Willis

HYGGE INSPIRATION

Chapter Six

SIMPLE PLEASURES

Hygge is about seeing beauty in the everyday and savoring each moment either in the form of well-deserved "me time" or spending time with loved ones. Take some time out to enjoy these simple pleasures and weave them into your life for a daily dose of hygge.

A Sumptuous
Candle-Lit Bath

A warm bath is one of the quickest ways to experience a blissful state of relaxation. Here's how to transform your bath into a therapeutic and nurturing spa retreat. Run your bath and add a handful of bath salts, which will help to soothe your muscles. Just before you get in, infuse the water with a few drops of calming essential oil, such as lavender, neroli, or rose. (It's best to mix the oil with a few tablespoons of olive oil first, as adding essential oils directly to hot water makes them evaporate quickly, so you lose their therapeutic benefits.) To nourish your skin, apply a face mask made from one mashed banana mixed with a tablespoon of orange juice and a tablespoon of honey. It smells good enough to eat but avoid the temptation! Then lie back and relax as the steam curls around you. For extra hygge, light some candles. After soaking for 20 minutes or so, step out of the bath, rinse your face with lukewarm water, and moisturize. Wrap yourself in your fluffiest bath robe and sit with a cup of herbal tea, read a good book, or take a well-deserved nap!

Reading by the Fire

What could be more relaxing than listening to the rain patter on the window as you sit by a crackling fire, immersed in a good book? Curl up with a ghost story, revel in a thriller, or revisit some childhood classics. Try reading aloud to someone you love as the fire gently flickers in the background. It's the perfect way to spend a cold, gray day or dark winter's evening.

Watch a Feel-Good Movie

One of the quickest ways to lift your spirits is to snuggle under a blanket or duvet and watch a feel-good movie. Whether you treat yourself to some blissful "me time" or huddle together with your family on the sofa with popcorn and drinks in hand, the following films are guaranteed to brighten your day!

Top ten feel-good movies:

- Pretty Woman
- It's a Wonderful Life
- Groundhog Day
- Dirty Dancing
- Little Miss Sunshine
- Amélie
- Forrest Gump
- Ferris Bueller's Day Off
- Back to the Future
- The Shawshank Redemption

Top ten family films:

- Ratatouille
- Frozen
- Shrek
- Up
- The Goonies
- E.T. the Extra-Terrestrial
- Toy Story
- Beauty and the Beast
- Wallace and Gromit: The Curse of the Were-Rabbit
- Any classic Walt Disney film (e.g., Pinocchio, Cinderella, Snow White and the Seven Dwarfs)

Playing Games with Friends

Search your attic and dust off your favorite board games. The dreariest day can be turned into a fun one by playing games around the fire with your nearest and dearest. Heat up some mulled wine, brew some fresh coffee, and pass around slices of homemade cake. Playing games the hyggelig way is all about connecting with the people in your life and focusing on having fun! Play a classic game such as Scrabble, Life, Backgammon, Monopoly, or Clue or test your physical and mental dexterity with Jenga!

Hygge Playlist

As Aldous Huxley said, "After silence, that which comes nearest to expressing the inexpressible is music." There is much to be said for the crackle of burning wood, the patter of rain on glass, and the crisp flick of pages turning, but they are not the only sounds that express hygge. It takes only a little rifling through your music collection to find tracks to accompany you in your exploration of the Scandinavian concept: there are songs that are the bite of the cold outdoors, songs that are the embrace of a loved one, and songs that are nights of quiet contemplation and contentment. Whatever lights your hygge candle, from blues and country to indie, jazz, and soul, you'll be able to find a hyggelig track on many of your favorite albums. Your hygge playlist can be the perfect accompaniment to other activities or you can simply lie back, close your eyes, and float on the eddies of the melody.

Fear less, hope more; eat less, chew more; whine less, breathe more; talk less, say more; hate less, love more; and all good things are yours.

—Scandinavian proverb